WELCOME TO THE WORLD OF
Hummingbirds

Diane Swanson

WALRUS
B O O K S

Edited by Elizabeth McLean
Cover design by Steve Penner
Interior design by Margaret Ng
Typeset by Jacqui Thomas
Photo research by Tanya Lloyd Kyi
Cover photograph by Anthony Mercieca/Dembinsky Photo Assoc
Photo credits: Alan G. Nelson/Dembinsky Photo Assoc iv; Anthony Mercieca/
Dembinsky Photo Assoc 2, 10, 12, 22, 24; Rob and Ann Simpson 4, 6, 14, 16, 18, 20, 26;
Dominique Braud/Dembinsky Photo Assoc 8

Printed and bound in Canada

Library and Archives Canada Cataloguing in Publication

Swanson, Diane, 1944–
    Welcome to the world of hummingbirds

    Includes index.
    ISBN 10: 1-55285-319-5 (bound). – ISBN 10: 1-55285-318-7 (pbk.)
    ISBN 13: 978-1-55285-319-1 (bound). – ISBN 13: 978-1-55285-318-4 (pbk.)

    1. Hummingbirds—North America—Juvenile literature. I. Title.
QL696.A558S92 2002   j598.7'64'097   C2002-910080-1

The publisher acknowledges the financial support of the Canada Council for the Arts, the British Columbia Arts Council, and the Government of Canada through the Book Publishing Industry Development Program (BPIDP). Whitecap Books also acknowledges the financial support of the Province of British Columbia through the Book Publishing Tax Credit.

BRITISH COLUMBIA
ARTS COUNCIL

Canada Council   Conseil des Ar
for the Arts   du Canada

Contents

World of Difference

Of all the birds
in North America,
the calliope
hummingbird
is the littlest.

HUMMMM...HUMMMM...HUMMMM.
It's much easier to hear hummingbird wings
than to see them. They beat so fast they
blur. But they're just what a hummer needs
to dart around fields, dipping its beak
into flowers to dine.

English-speaking people named
hummingbirds after the hum of their
beating wings, but people who spoke
Portuguese focused on the way the birds
feed. Their word for hummingbird means
"kiss the flower." The French seemed
especially struck by its little body, naming
it "fly-sized bird."

1

A blue-throated hummingbird shines in the light.

Hummers are the smallest birds in the world. The calliope hummingbird is the tiniest in North America. Full-grown, it is as short as your thumb and weighs less than a penny.

The calliope is one of approximately 340 different kinds of hummingbirds. North America, including Mexico, is home to about 50 kinds.

All hummingbirds wear thick coats. For their size, they produce more feathers than any other bird. And on many hummers, some of these feathers gleam like colorful jewels in bright sunshine. Stand between a hummingbird and the sun— with the light to your back— and you'll witness the flash as the bird faces the sun. WOW! But when the light or the angle isn't right, the brilliance disappears, and bright colors fade to drab.

HATS OFF TO HUMMINGBIRDS

Hummers are awesome. Here are some of the reasons why:

- Three broad-tailed hummingbird chicks—newly hatched—weigh only as much as a single paper clip.
- One blue-throated humming-bird nest, used for 10 years, contained 24 000 kilometres (15 000 miles) of spider silk.
- Some hummingbirds carry hitchhikers. Mites catch rides in their nostrils, then race down their beaks to feed on flowers.

Where in the World

HUMMINGBIRDS LIVE WHERE FLOWERS BLOOM—but only in the western half of the world. The birds all make their homes in North, Central, and South America. Most kinds live in hot jungles. Others do well in cooler climates. Rufous hummingbirds, for instance, spend part of each year in Alaska.

Look for hummingbirds of one kind or another in very different types of homes: sea coasts, forests, mountain meadows, deserts, and grassy plains. The birds raise their families in the wilderness, but also in busy city parks and backyard gardens.

A mass of honeysuckle flowers attracts a hungry hummingbird.

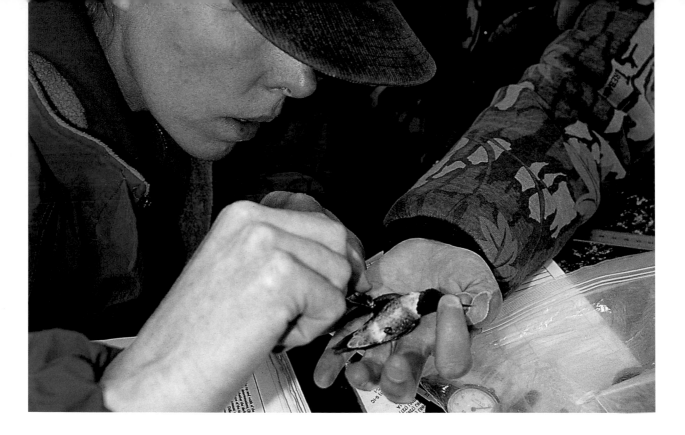

Hummingbirds are banded so researchers can study them more easily.

If you set out a feeder of sugary water, hummingbirds will often arrive for dinner. Some become so comfortable around people, they perch on fingers to eat.

Hummingbirds have territories, areas they defend as their own. Many kinds will challenge an invader head-on. Usually it's the invader that takes off.

Twice each year, a few kinds of hummingbirds migrate long distances between their summer and winter homes. Ruby-throated and rufous hummers fly more than 3200 kilometres (2000 miles) from their nesting sites in the north to their winter homes in the south. About 800 kilometres (500 miles) of the ruby-throated's long journey is across the Gulf of Mexico. It's an amazing trip, which the hummingbirds make nonstop, and usually alone.

TAGGED FOR TRACKING

Spot hummingbirds wearing bracelets and you'll have found birds tagged by researchers. Scientists are trying to learn more about where the birds travel and how long they live.

Being tagged doesn't seem to bother the hummingbirds. They're held gently while tiny bands are snapped around their legs. The date and the numbers on the bands are recorded, then the birds are released—all within minutes. One rufous tagged in British Columbia turned up in New Mexico just six weeks later.

World Full of Food

IMAGINE EATING SIX TIMES AN HOUR. That's nothing for a hummingbird. It normally feeds every 10 minutes— sometimes more often—downing about 60 meals a day!

Hummingbirds are so active they burn up energy fast. One scientist figured that if an average man used as much energy as a ruby-throated hummingbird, he would need to eat 130 kilograms (285 pounds) of hamburger every day. And before the ruby-throated migrates, it stores energy by eating even more than usual, growing about 50 percent heavier. The extra weight slows

Feeding from this trumpetlike bloom is no problem for a ruby-throated hummer.

9

Tree sap oozing from holes left by sapsuckers makes a meal for a rufous hummingbird.

its speed, but it helps the bird fly farther.

A hummingbird feeds mostly on nectar—the sweet liquid formed inside flowers. The bird sticks its long tongue into a blossom and laps the nectar. The liquid rises through grooves along the tongue. Then the bird draws its tongue back in. Its beak squeezes the nectar off when the bird sticks its tongue out again. To get enough food, a hummer might need to check out 3000 blossoms in a single day.

The fringed, split tip of the tongue of many kinds of hummingbirds can pick up meals of insects and spiders along with the nectar. The birds also catch insects in flight and snatch spiders from their webs.

Some kinds, such as ruby-throated and Anna's humming-birds, feast on sweet tree sap, too. They lunch at holes drilled through the bark by wood-peckers called sapsuckers.

PAYING THEIR WAY

Hummingbirds serve the plants that feed them. When the birds poke their tongues into a blossom, powdery pollen sticks to their heads. Then it rubs off on the next blossom. Most flowers need the pollen from other blooms to produce seeds.

Mountain flowers called paintbrushes depend almost completely on hummingbirds to spread pollen. The blossoms don't attract insect pollinators such as honeybees because the nectar is too deep for them to reach.

11

World in Motion

WALKING ISN'T FOR HUMMINGBIRDS. Their legs aren't built for the job. The birds might shuffle along a branch, but even for short stretches such as that, they're much more likely to fly.

Hummingbirds are most at home in the air. They're champion acrobats of the sky! Not only can they zoom forward like other birds, they can also go backward. As they move from flower to flower, they flit sideways easily. If flying upside down might help the hummers escape danger, they can do that, too—for short distances. But most amazingly of all, they can hover in midair.

Like other hummingbirds, this Costa's hummer rarely uses its tiny legs to travel.

13

Narrow, pointed wings help make these acrobatics possible. The wings are strong, too. The muscles that move them weigh at least one-quarter as much as the whole bird. And the hummingbird moves its wings in an odd way, tracing figure eights in the air. That helps it create power on both the upbeat and the downbeat. Depending on the kind

A hummingbird beats its wings too fast to be seen clearly.

of hummer and what it's doing, it often beats its wings more than 40 times a second!

For its size, the hummingbird travels at a quick pace. The ruby-throated has been tracked at 43 kilometres (27 miles) an hour. It flies—and dives—much faster when it's trying to attract a mate or respond to threats. But traveling at full speed doesn't end in crash landings. A hummer can make sudden stops—even on a narrow perch—with grace.

Like you, hummingbirds rest at night. But if the air is cold—day or night—they enter a deep sleep called torpor. Heart and breathing rates drop sharply, and body temperatures fall to just above air temperatures. This deathlike sleep helps the birds survive by saving energy.

The trouble is that hummers can't escape danger until they come out of torpor. An Anna's hummingbird, for instance, must wait to fly until its body warms to about 30°C (86°F).

World of Words

SHOWING OFF IS ONE WAY TO SEND SIGNALS. During mating seasons, male hummingbirds use fancy flying to tell females they want to mate. Each kind has its own style. Ruby-throated males often sweep back and forth in front of the females. Lucifers spiral upward, then plunge straight back down. Black-chinned males perform figure eights, over and over again.

Many hummingbirds deliver these high-flying signals in bright sunshine where their throat feathers "light up." The flashing is another sign of their interest.

Some, such as male Costa's hummers,

A male black-chinned hummer displays his colors, attracting the eye of a female.

"Go away!"
A female rufous
hummingbird
tries to scare
off a jay.

add sound to their showy flights. They dive
so fast the air whistles through their feathers.
Broad-tailed hummers tri-l-l-l-l when air
speeds through slots formed by the narrow
tips on a few of their feathers. Some male
hummingbirds also sing to their mates by
twittering, squeaking, or clicking.

So what's the female response to all this

talk? Anna's hummers express their interest by fluffing up their feathers, wiggling their heads, and squeaking. Then they fly off to the nests they're building—with the males after them. White-eared females also lead males to their nesting areas.

Once there, a female might fly from perch to perch, followed by a male. They also take flights together, now and then hovering beak to beak. It's a way of saying, "Let's mate."

GET THE MESSAGE?

Hummingbirds face many dangers. Fish and frogs sometimes grab the birds when they're near water. Nectar-feeding orioles might fight them for flowers. Jays, snakes, and squirrels often eat their eggs or chicks.

Still, as small as they are, hummingbirds use bold body language to scare off many of their enemies. The little birds charge them, diving from the heights with their spearlike—though weak—beaks. The message is unmistakable: SCRAM!

19

World of Nests

MOSS, FUNGUS, BLOSSOMS, AND BARK—even hair and lint from clothes. They're all things hummingbirds can use to build their nests. But there's something else the birds need: silk from spider webs. One of the strongest fibers on Earth, the silk helps hold the nests together and anchors them firmly in place.

It's the female hummingbirds that build the nests, starting soon after—or just before—they mate. Hovering over the material they've gathered, several kinds of hummingbirds press it with their chests, giving it a cuplike shape. Then they add linings of soft matter,

A hummer's nest blends well with its surroundings.

21

Two tiny eggs sit snugly inside a hummingbird's nest.

such as the fluff from dandelion seeds.

The nests vary in size and location, depending on the builder. A ruby-throated hummingbird creates a nest as small as a walnut, while a broad-tailed hummer builds one a bit deeper and wider. Tiny calliopes often nest on or near pine cones, making their homes nearly impossible to notice.

Blue-throated hummingbirds sometimes find safe nesting spots under bridges, in barns, or on the eaves of houses. Some hummers use a good nest over and over again.

Although Anna's hummingbirds might nest in winter, most hummers wait until spring. Then they lay two white eggs about the size of peas. Within their firm, thick nests, the female birds care for their eggs until they both hatch. The hummers leave only for short periods to feed.

The folks at the Arizona–Sonora Desert Museum were just trying to improve their live hummingbird display. They hauled out the old plants, enlarged the space, then replanted it. Soon, the birds started nesting again. But the homes they built were too loose. Many collapsed, and the eggs they held fell out.

Museum managers were puzzled until they realized they'd cleaned out all the spiders—and the silk webs that hummingbirds need to bind their nests.

New World

A HUMMER KEEPS BUSY ON THE NEST. A female hummer, that is. Using her long beak, she carefully turns her eggs over every few hours. That helps keep them evenly warm as she presses her body against them.

About two weeks later, the humming-bird feels something: tap, tap, tap. The chicks peck away inside their eggs. Hour after hour they work, until finally the shells crack open.

Like many other kinds of birds, humming-bird chicks start life without feathers or sight. It takes a couple of weeks or more

25

Hummers like this broad-billed hummingbird learn to groom themselves with their beaks.

before they grow coats and open their eyes. So it's a good thing their mother looks after them. After she feeds herself, she returns to the nest and pokes her beak down the chicks' throats. It looks as if she's hurting the young birds, but she's not. It's her way of pumping some of the food she's eaten directly into the chicks.

When little hummers are only two to three weeks old, they start flying. They're surprisingly good right away, but they have to work to improve their landing skills. Then they can follow their mother from flower to flower and learn to feed as she does. The chicks also practice chasing and catching insects in the air. Sometimes, they chase each other, too—just for fun.

All hummingbird chicks must struggle to survive. If they're lucky, they may live about five or more years.

WATER ROMP

If you've ever dashed through the spray from a lawn sprinkler, you'll know what attracts hummingbirds to hoses. They seem to enjoy the short showers that also keep them clean. Sometimes they dive and roll in the water, riding it as it rises.

At quieter times, hummingbirds bathe in slow-flowing streams—usually in shallow water along the banks. Then they fly to the branches of bushes or trees and shake their feathers dry.

Index

Collect all Welcome to the World titles

- [ ] Welcome to the World of Wolves
- [ ] Welcome to the World of Whales
- [ ] Welcome to the World of Bears
- [ ] Welcome to the World of Otters
- [ ] Welcome to the World of Owls
- [ ] Welcome to the World of Wild Cats
- [ ] Welcome to the World of Eagles
- [ ] Welcome to the World of Foxes
- [ ] Welcome to the World of Bats
- [ ] Welcome to the World of Raccoons
- [ ] Welcome to the World of Beavers
- [ ] Welcome to the World of Spirit Bears
- [ ] Welcome to the World of Skunks
- [ ] Welcome to the World of Porcupines
- [ ] Welcome to the World of Octopuses

- [ ] Welcome to the World of Rabbits and Hares
- [ ] Welcome to the World of Sharks
- [ ] Welcome to the World of Snakes
- [ ] Welcome to the World of Squirrels
- [ ] Welcome to the World of Coyotes
- [ ] Welcome to the World of Wild Horses
- [ ] Welcome to the World of Hummingbirds
- [ ] Welcome to the World of Frogs and Toads
- [ ] Welcome to the World of Alligators and Crocodiles
- [ ] Welcome to the World of Elephants
- [ ] Welcome to the World of Penguins
- [ ] Welcome to the World of Orangutans
- [ ] Welcome to the World of Kangaroos
- [ ] Welcome to the World of Wolverines
- [ ] Welcome to the World of Moose

Did you know there are approximately 340 different kinds of hummingbirds, some as light as a penny? These champion acrobats of the sky can beat their wings more than 40 times a second, fly backward and even hover in midair, like helicopters. Since it's much easier to hear hummingbird wings than see them, just follow the hum to find these birds!

Collect the Series

CDN $6.95
US $5.95

COVER PHOTOGRAPH: ANTHONY MERCIECA/DEMBINSKY PHOTO ASSOC
COVER DESIGN: STEVE PENNER

whitecap | www.whitecap.ca

ISBN 978-1-55285-318-4
50595
480
$5.95
84